Piano Solo

Best of Suzanne Ciani

CONTENTS

Anthem 3

Berceuse 9

Butterflies 14

Celtic Nights 23

Dentecane 32

For Lise 37

Full Moon Sonata 42

Go Gently 49

La Mer 54

Meeting Mozart 66

Pretend 59

Snow Crystals 72

Sogno Agitato 79

Turning 86

The Velocity of Love .92

Photos by Terri Gold

ISBN-13: 978-1-4234-1782-8
ISBN-10: 1-4234-1782-8

HAL•LEONARD®
CORPORATION
7777 W. BLUEMOUND RD. P.O. BOX 13819 MILWAUKEE, WI 53213

Visit Hal Leonard Online at
www.halleonard.com

Suzanne Ciani is one of the world's leading New Age composers and performers. She has been called a "female Chopin" and *Keyboard Magazine*'s "New Age Keyboardist of the Year." She is best loved for her 15 albums of original music, which have garnered prestigious awards, including 5 GRAMMY® nominations, three Indie nominations and an Indie Award for Best New Age Album.

Her music communicates the special intimacy, passion, and sensitivity that have become her trademark and prompted fans to buy over a million of her albums.

Ciani is a graduate of Wellesley College and holds a Masters in Music Composition from the University of California at Berkeley.

To learn more about Suzanne Ciani, please visit her website at **www.suzanneciani.com**.

A message from Suzanne

Dear Pianist,

Thank you for sharing this music with me.

I hope that you feel the joy I feel while playing "Butterflies," the introspection of "Pretend," the sensuality of "La Mer," the angst of "Sogno Agitato," the peacefulness of "Berceuse," the reverence of "Meeting Mozart," and the triumph of "Anthem."

When I play, I let the music transport me, entering into the mood and energy of the piece. A rhythmic steadiness, providing undercurrents of peacefulness and strength, is often an element of my musical style, perhaps because of a childhood love of baroque music and partly because of a long and exclusive devotion to analog synthesis and sequencers. I also have a fascination for counterpoint and it is important to bring out the inner voices.

It was hard to choose for this book—I wish it could have been twice as long. Almost half of the pieces are never before published. Most can be heard on my solo piano recordings, Pianissimo I, II and III.

Recently I was very moved to hear someone playing one of my pieces with a sensitivity and skill that moved me to tears...and I have heard performances where I barely recognized the music as mine.

I give you these written notes, but notes do not music make—musicality is the gift of the performing musician.

Thank you for your gifts.

ANTHEM

*I have dedicated "Anthem" to the Chinese students in
Tiennenman Square on June 4, 1989 – in celebration of their spirit and commitment.*

By SUZANNE CIANI

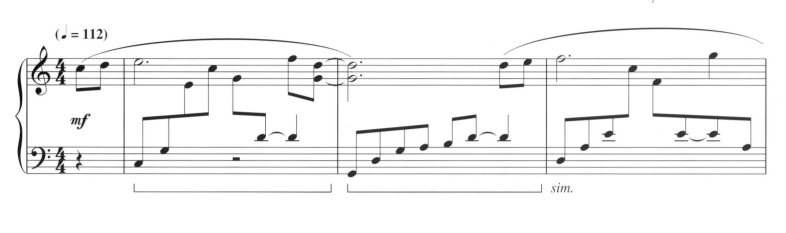

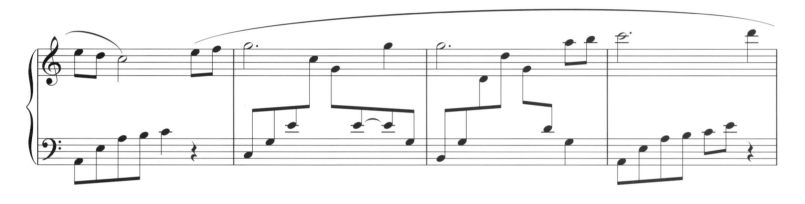

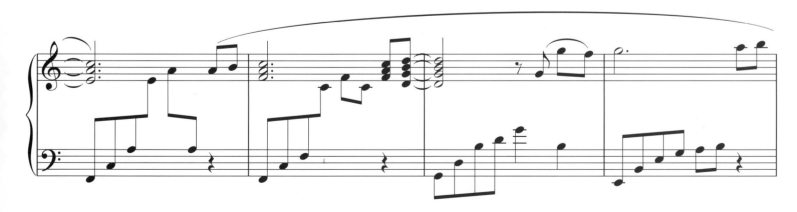

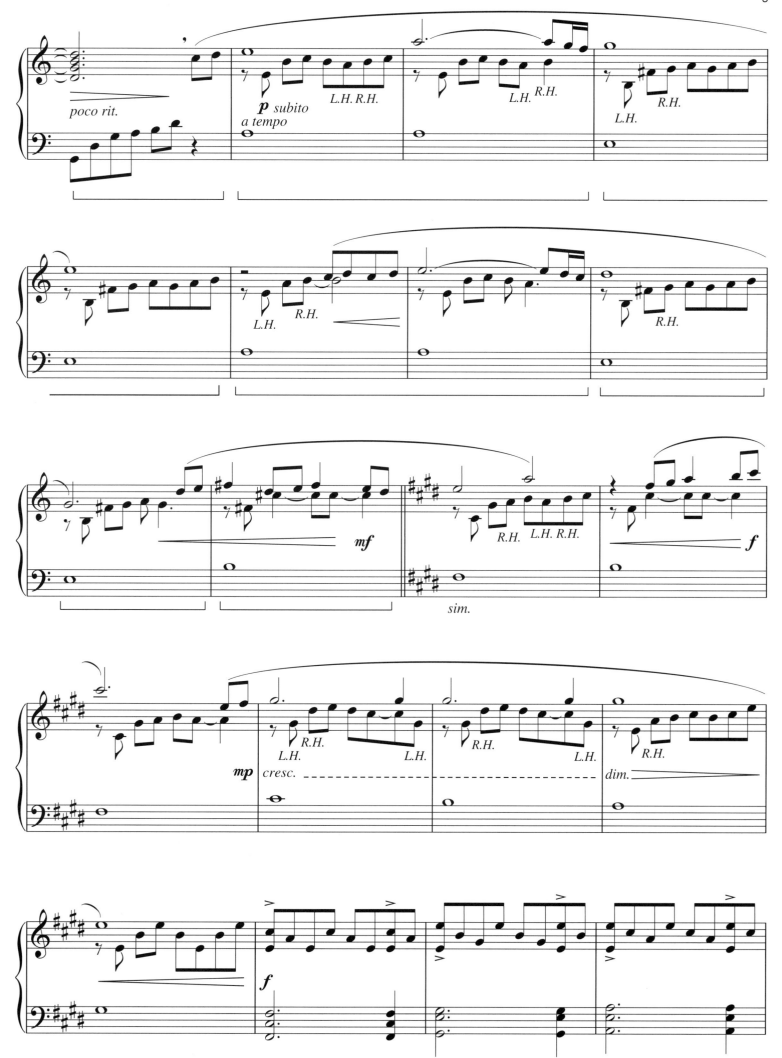

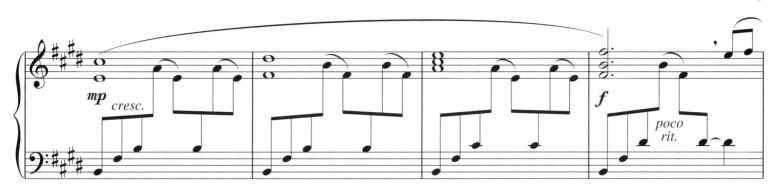

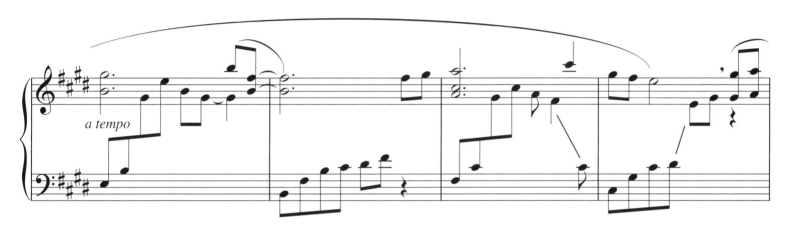
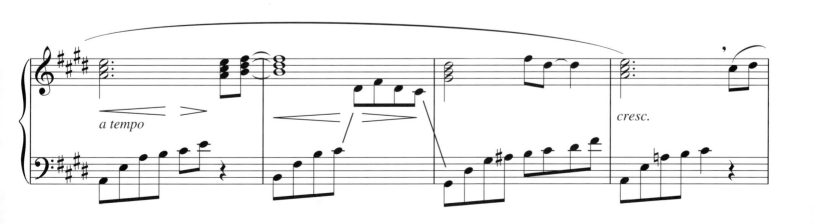

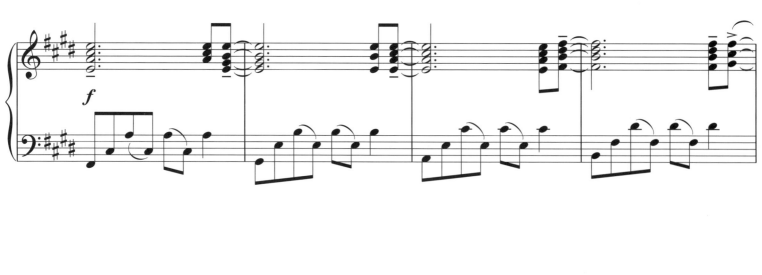

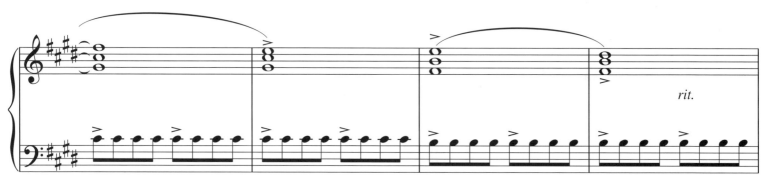

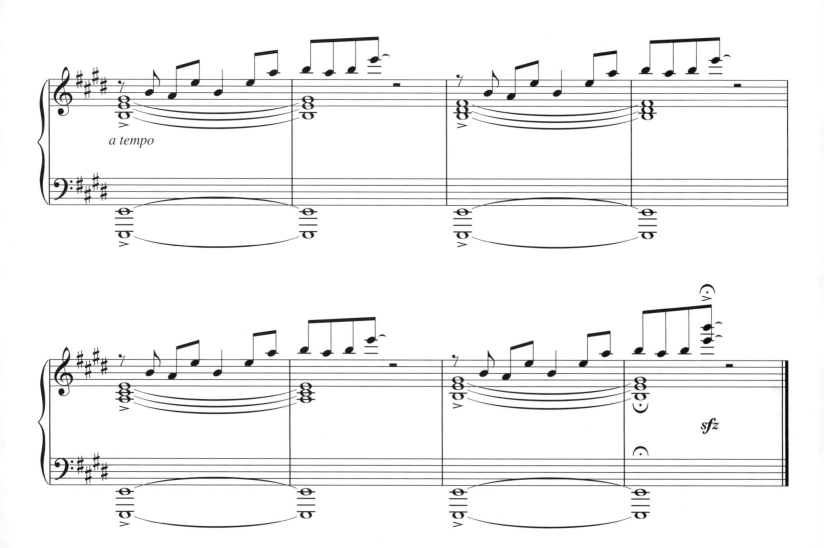

BERCEUSE

In memory of my dear cousin Amy

By SUZANNE CIANI

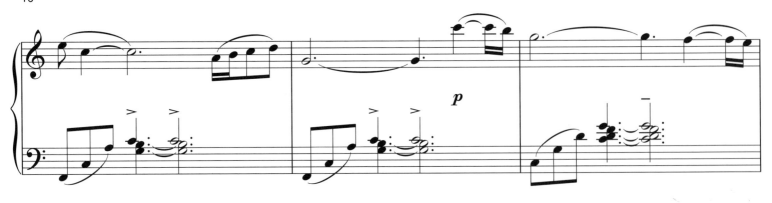

BUTTERFLIES

Once a year the monarchs come in fluttering droves.

By SUZANNE CIANI

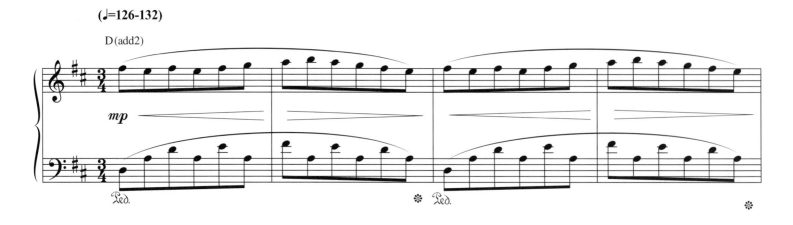

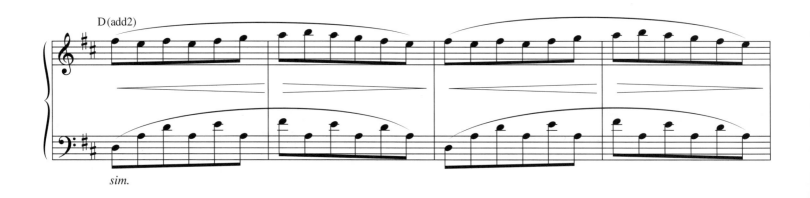

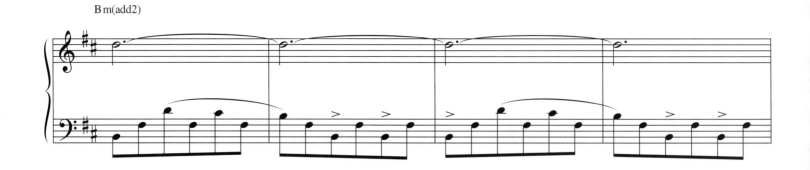

CELTIC NIGHTS

By SUZANNE CIANI

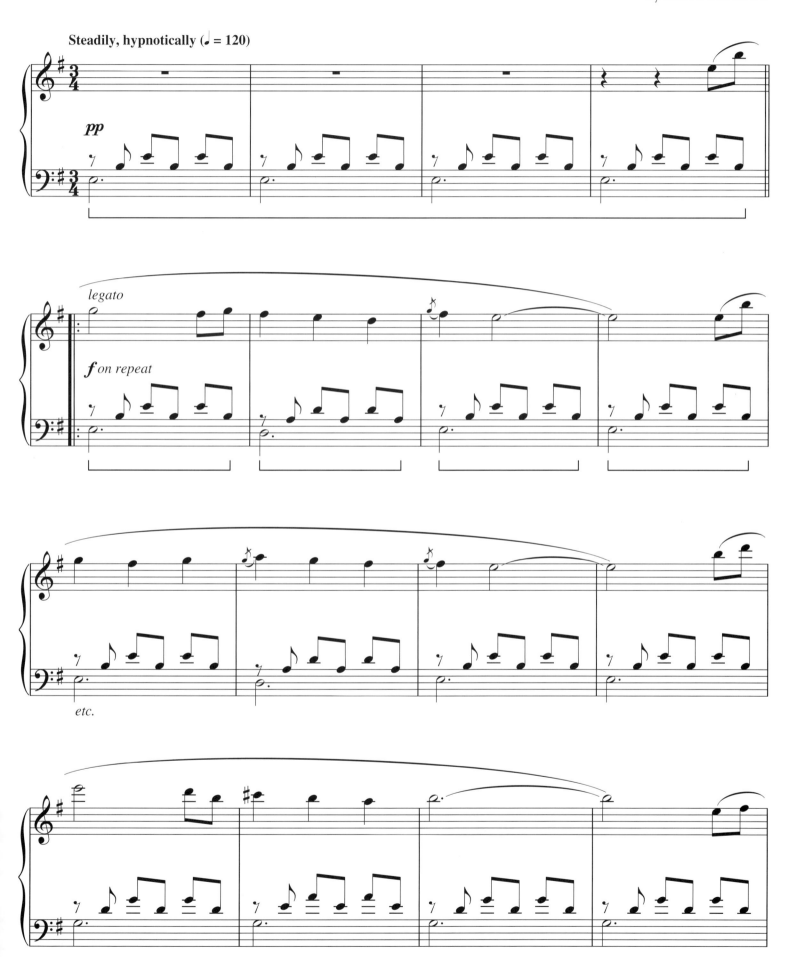

With improvisational freedom (left hand steady, right hand need not be steady)

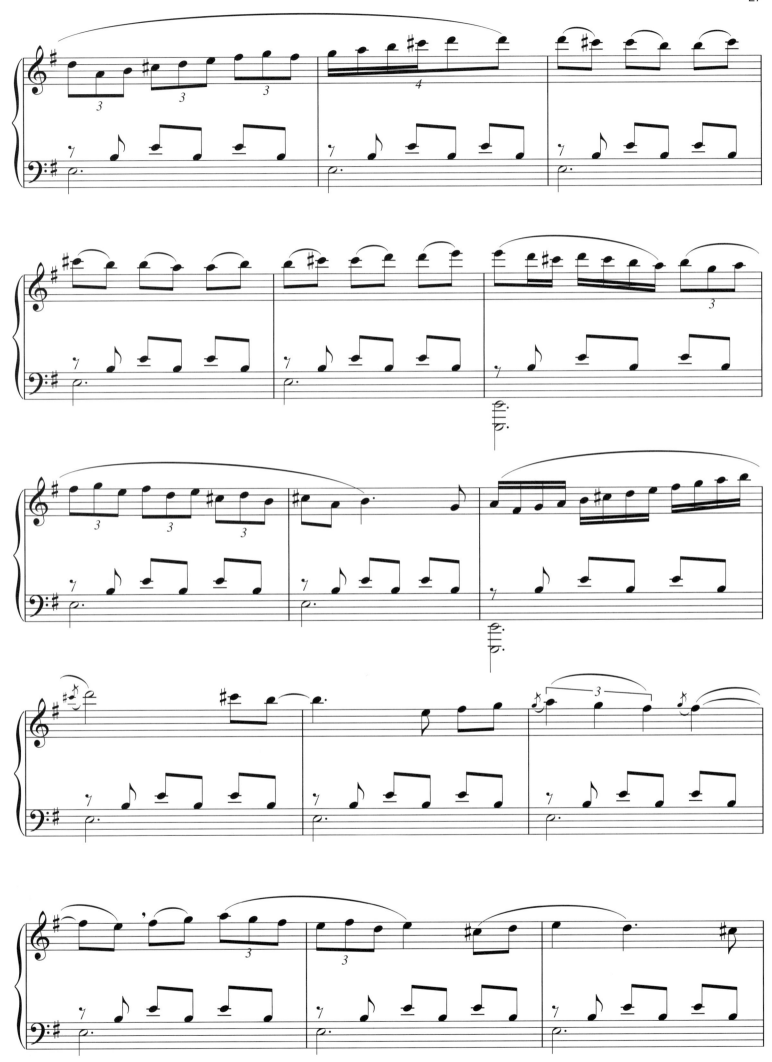

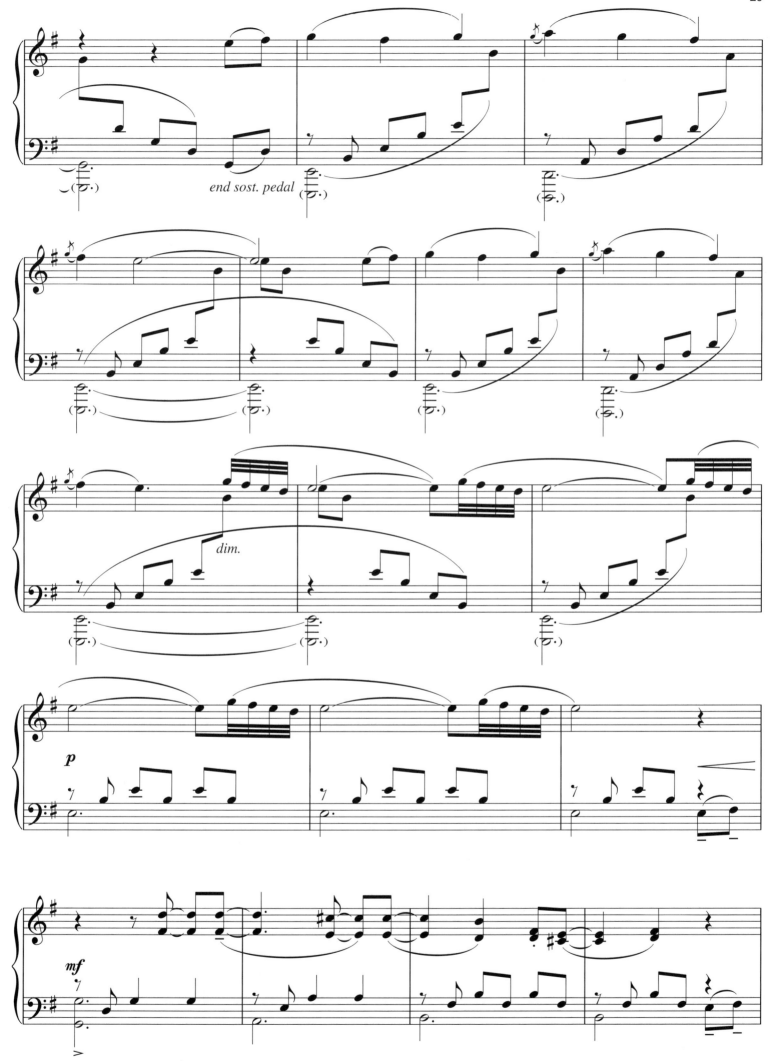

DENTECANE

The small town in Italy where Silver Ship began...

By SUZANNE CIANI

Pensively, with rubato

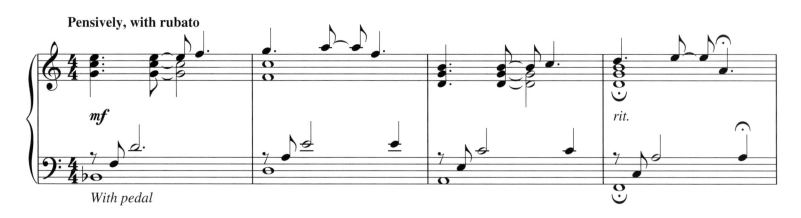

With pedal

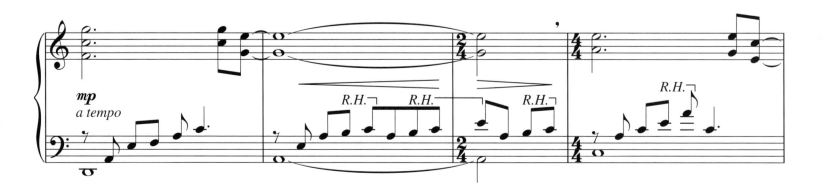

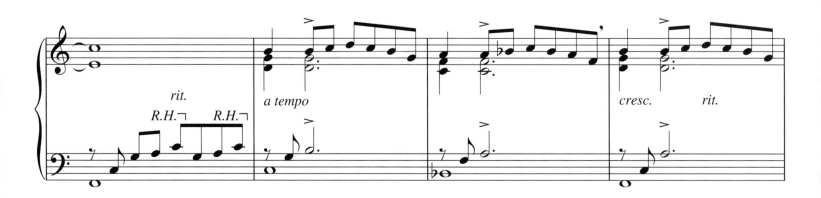

FOR LISE

for Lise in memory of Tasha

By SUZANNE CIANI

FULL MOON SONATA

… pulled into dreaming by the magnetic moonlight

By SUZANNE CIANI

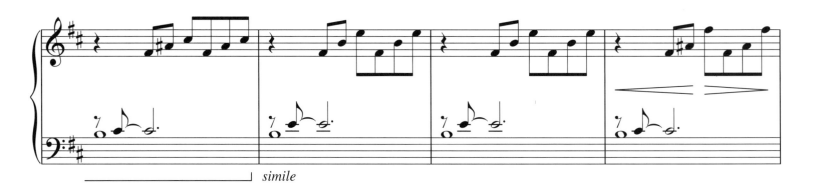

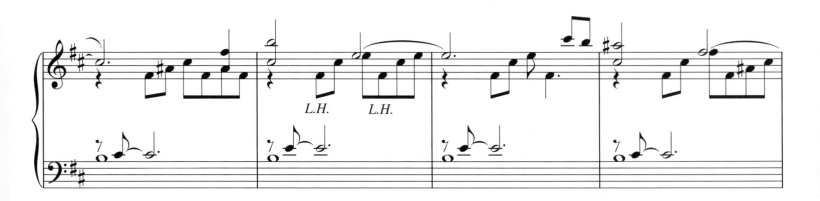

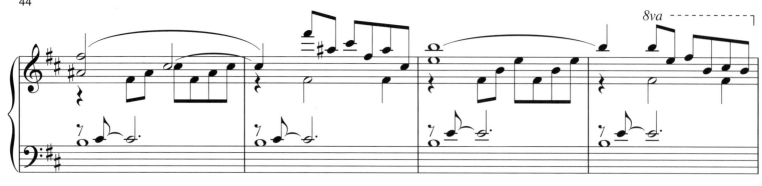

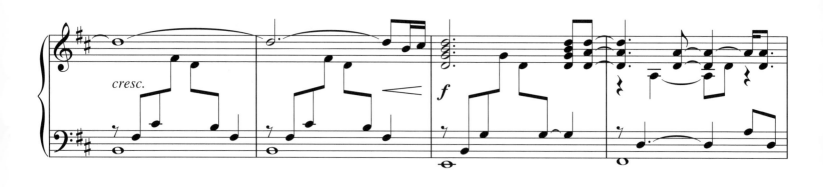

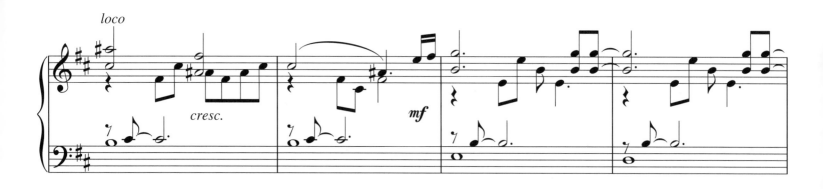

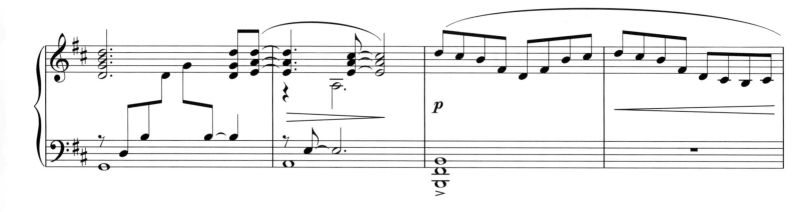

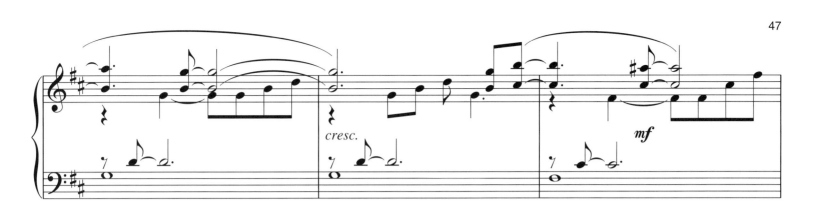

GO GENTLY

For my father, Dr. A. Walter Ciani

By SUZANNE CIANI
and JEREMY LUBBOCK

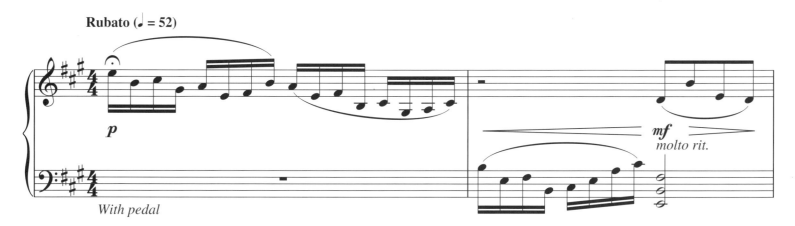

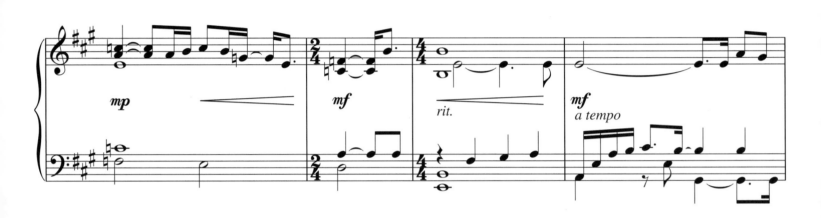

LA MER

The sea is music — for me, for Debussy, for Ravel, forever.

By SUZANNE CIANI

PRETEND

The afterimage of someone gone...

By SUZANNE CIANI

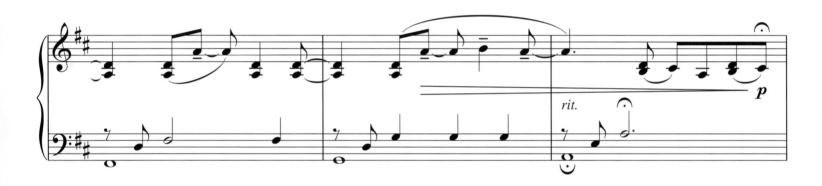

MEETING MOZART

…and in the palace anteroom, I met Mozart…

By SUZANNE CIANI

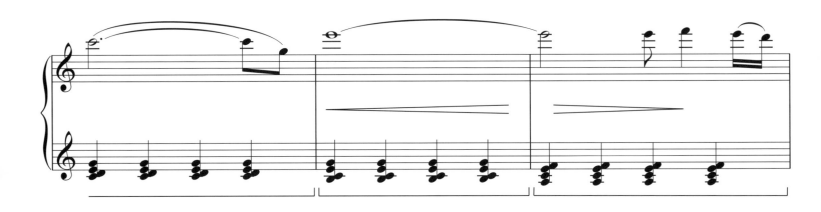

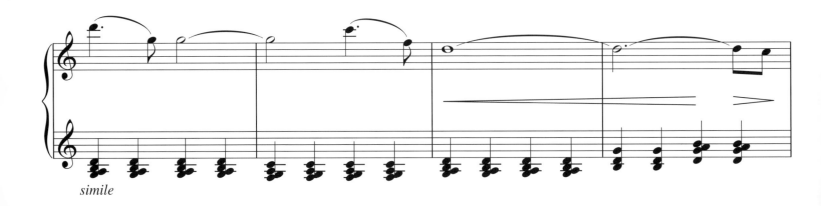

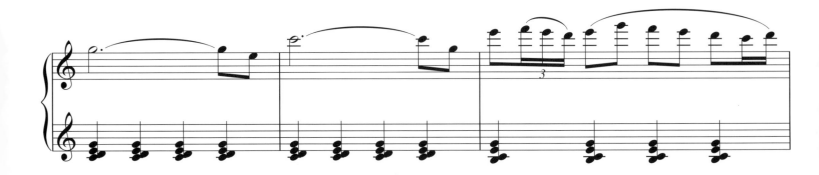

To Coda ⊕

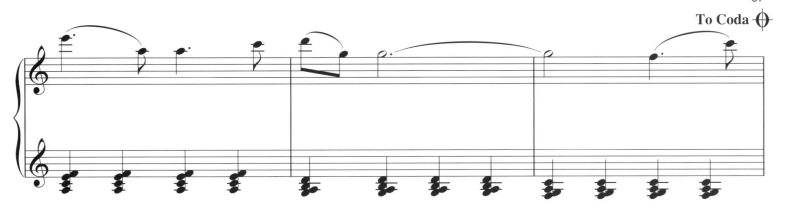

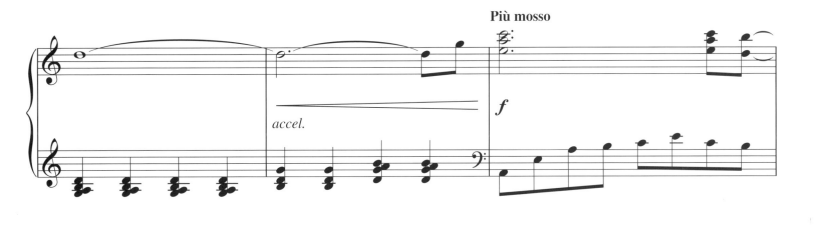

SNOW CRYSTALS

The wonder of ever-changing dancing snowflakes

By SUZANNE CIANI

74

SOGNO AGITATO

In Italian, even the word for nightmare sounds beautiful.

By SUZANNE CIANI

With passion (♩=130)

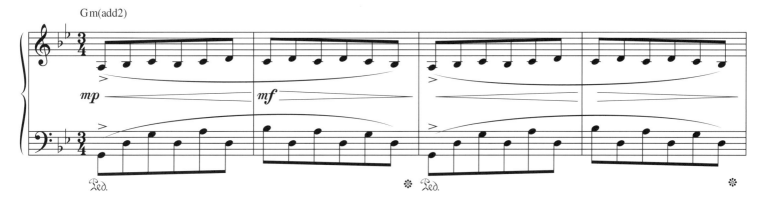

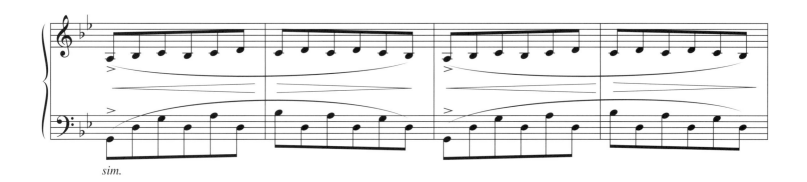

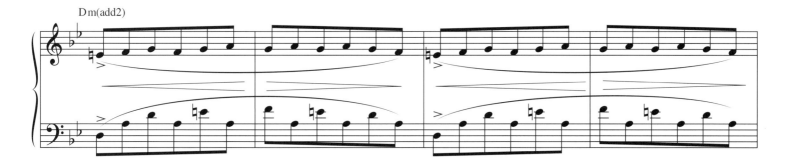

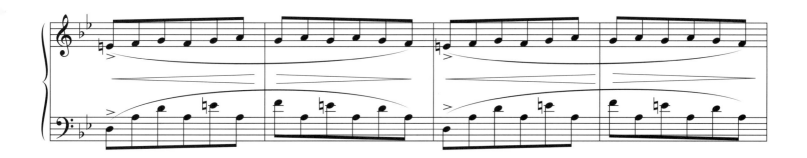

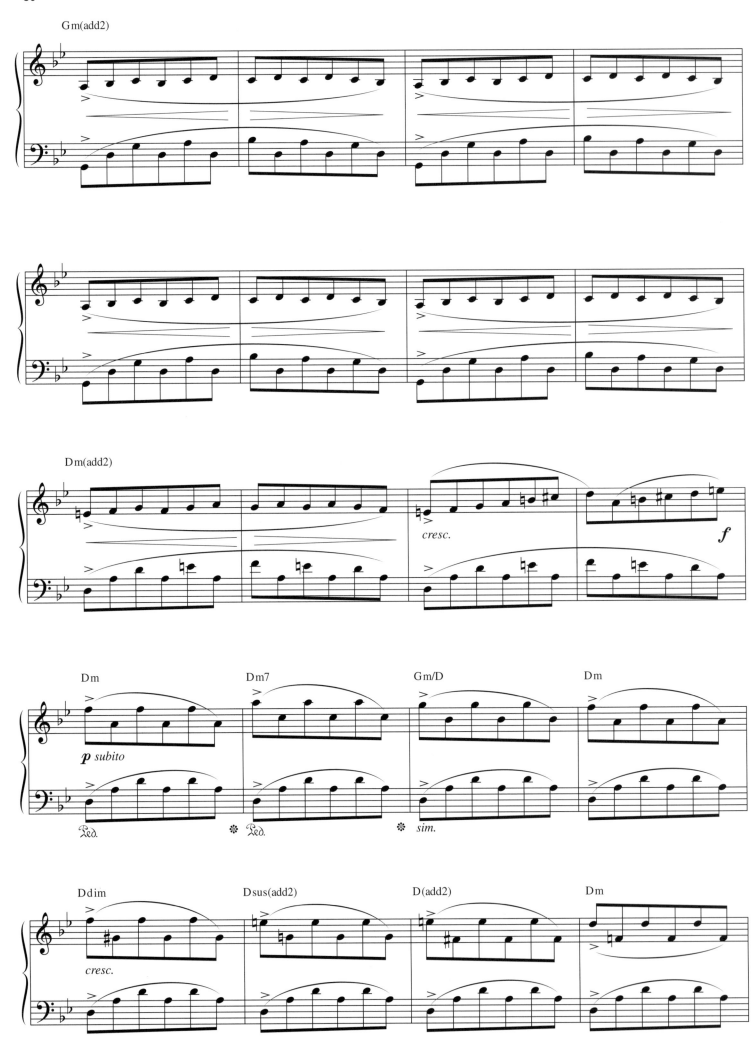

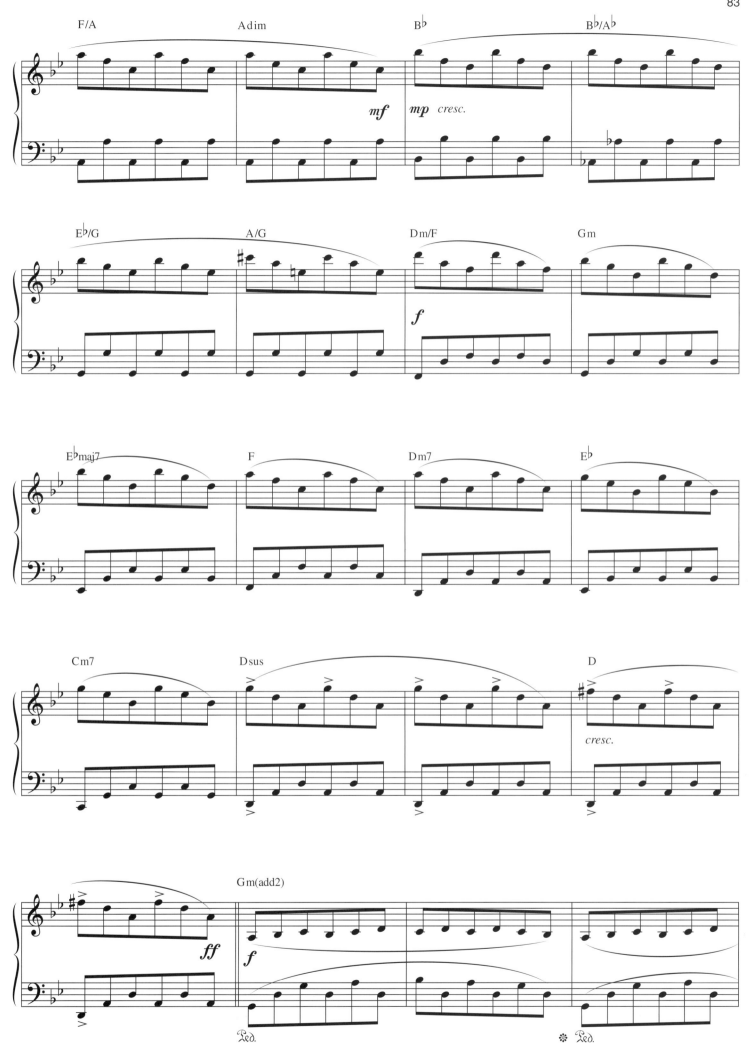

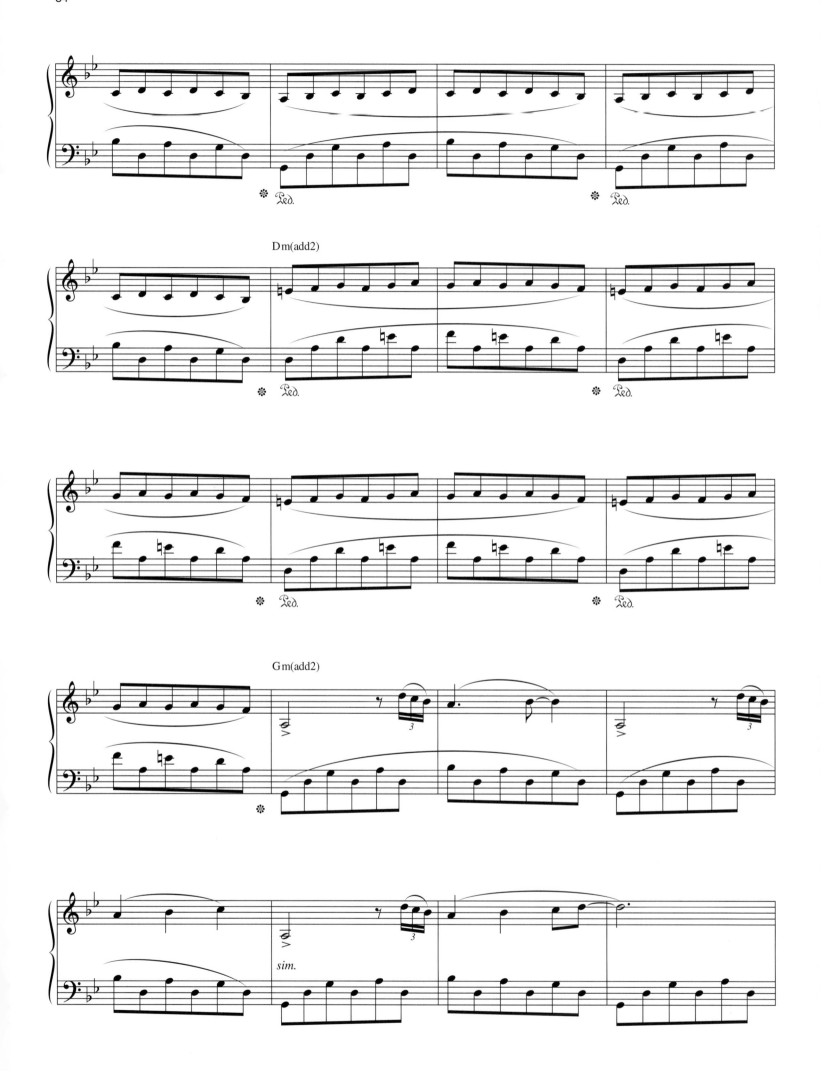

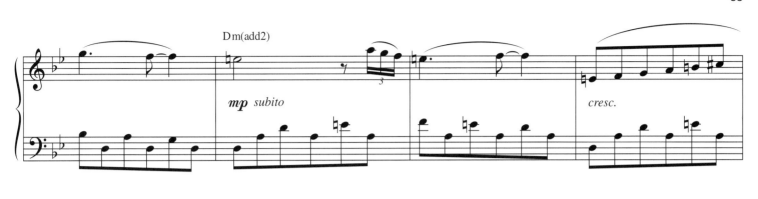

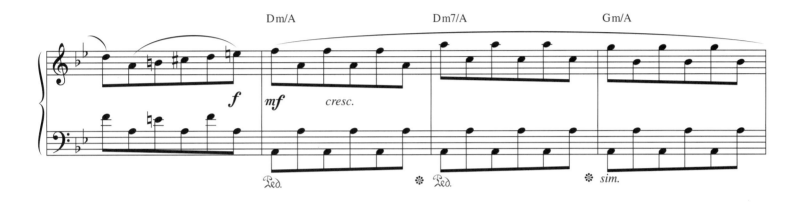

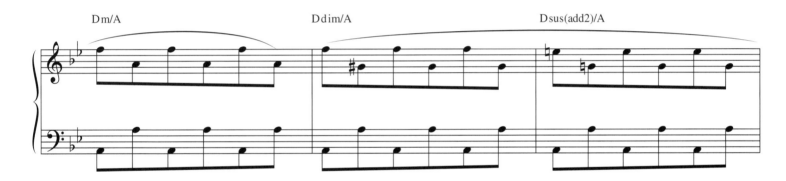

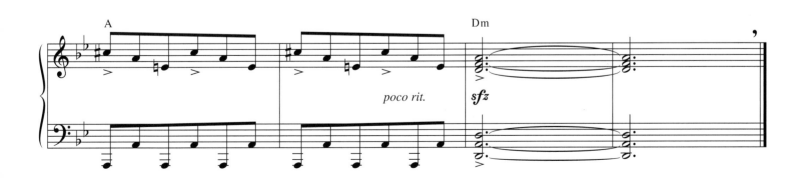

TURNING

Turn like the seasons, Turn back to me once again...

By SUZANNE CIANI

89

2nd time both hands 8va

mp

THE VELOCITY OF LOVE

Slowly, slowly, with the velocity of love...

By SUZANNE CIANI

With pedal

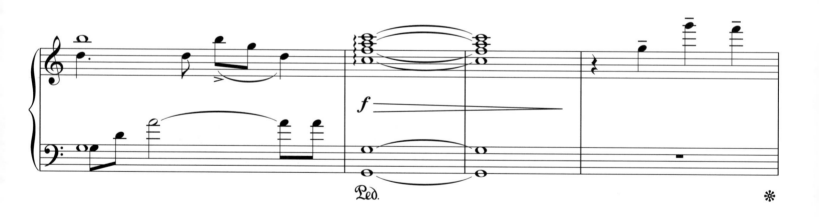